THE INCLUSION OF WOMEN IN PEACE BUILDING IN WEST AFRICA:

CRITICAL LOOK AT WOMEN'S CONTRIBUTION IN PEACE BUILDING AND NEGOTIATIONS.

by

Ndey Jobarteh

THE INCLUSION OF WOMEN IN PEACE BUILDING IN WEST AFRICA

Dedication

This is dedicated to African women who had contributed and took leadership in peace building both at community and international level.

Table of Contents

Preface

There is a rising awareness on the role, inclusion and importance of women in Peace building and negotiation at all levels. The number of women participating in formal peace processes remains relatively very small and in some cases absent from internationally peace processes, where negotiation takes place. A classic case is the Ivorian Peace Negotiation where there was only one woman after the women in Ivorian had struggle so hard to get the two warring factions to the negotiating table.

This book aims to examine the effects of conflict on women and their major contributions to the quest for peace in the Mano River Region, West Africa. The paper will trace the strategies used by women in building peace, those conditions in women's lives which are unfavorable to its realization, and thus the need to involve them in peace-building. Emphasis will be placed on women organisations engage in peace-building in the Mano River Region. Additionally, it will discuss the challenges that women face, strategies for addressing the challenges and the importance of women's inclusion in peace building in creating a sustainable peace in Africa.

Introduction

Over the past twenty years, millions of Africans have lost their lives in wars and genocide. Many more have become refugees. Twenty-one out of fifty-four African countries are affected by conflict. Conflicts in Africa have meant a steady flow of resources towards sustaining these wars and away from building the infrastructure the continent so badly needs.

Since the late 1980's, West Africa has been the hotbed of protracted inter and intra state conflicts with multi-layered and intricate causes. The Mano River Union region has experienced the brunt of these conflicts, with millions being killed, internally displaced and dislocated in Liberia, Sierra Leone, Cote d'Ivoire, Guinea Bissau and many internal conflicts. These conflicts saw the increase in strength of rebel armies fighting for economic and political exclusion against State structures leading to widespread insecurity not only for inhabitants of the affected states but all nations in the region. While conflict inflicts suffering on everyone, women are particularly affected by its short- and long-term effects. Sexual assault and exploitation are frequently employed as tools of war; victimization leads to isolation, alienation, prolonged emotional trauma, and unwanted pregnancies that often result in abandoned children (USAID, 2007). These conflicts have therefore placed tremendous burdens on women who suffer displacement, loss of families and livelihoods, various forms of intense, gender-based violence, and the responsibility of sustaining entire communities.

Gender based violence is not an accident or inevitable by product of conflict. In this century it has been used as a deliberate and systematic tool to annihilate or subdue entire communities through the use of women's bodies as an integral part of the battlefield. There is growing evidence to suggest that gender based violence increases at times of social and political instability, either because men feel helpless to protect families and communities which leads to violence, or where men feel that gender based violence inflicted on 'their women' at the hands of the 'enemy' has dishonored the family. This in turn leads to the infliction of further violence or abandonment of women to preserve family honour or as punishment (Lata Narayanaswamy and Charlie Sever, 2004). The physical damage will take many years to heal. The psychological and spiritual damage is everlasting. Millions of African women live their lives in refugee camps as hell on earth. Lack of security, sexual exploitation, lack of opportunities all converge to make victims out of those who could otherwise have been called survivors. Women and children from countries such as Liberia, Rwanda, Sudan, Sierra Leone, Democratic Republic of Congo, Angola, Burundi and Somalia have spent the last decade living under unbelievably difficult circumstances.

As these conflicts metamorphosed gaining new actors and boundaries, it became clear that State apparatus could not sufficiently cope with the consequences alone. The quest for homegrown solutions became prevalent and the contributions of non-state actors to the very survival of West Africa states became urgent. Thus, since the early 1990s civil society groups at community, national and regional levels have been embarking on initiatives aimed at mitigating violent conflicts and building peace. Civil society's participation is based on the rationale that in order to create sustainable peace, the capacities and interests of all stakeholders must be taken into account, with particular regard to the capabilities and concerns at the grassroots level. However, the role of women as key stakeholders in peace have been underutilized and/or undermined. This is due to the fact that war and peace are highly gendered activities.

Women and men not only have different access to power structures and material resources before, during and after the escalation of a conflict; they also experience the pre-conflict phase, the open conflict, and the post-conflict situation in rather different ways. At the same time violent conflicts and wars in Africa are patriarchal activities, which illuminate what is masculine and feminine in society. While it is predominantly boys and men who go to the frontlines to fight, it is widely acknowledged that women are vulnerable targets of various forms of violence during wars such as rape, forced prostitution and more tragic the spread of HIV/AIDS. "Wars and armed conflicts generate fertile conditions for the spread of HIV. Rape inside or outside refugee camps has doubtless played a part in spreading the virus" (UNAIDS 1998).

While it is true that women suffer disproportionately during violent conflicts and wars, the description of women solely as victims ignores the vital roles they play in either preventing the outbreak of violence or building post-conflict communities. Viewing women either as helpless victims or a resourceful and stoic group struggling to take care of their families not only simplifies the significant differences between women and men, but also results in ill-equipped programmes and policies that are based on these distorted generalizations and therefore fail to address the actual needs of women(Pankhurst, D, 2000).

This situation has created a hierarchy in peacetime where men are relied upon to develop frameworks and strategies for rebuilding war torn societies. The exclusion of women from decision-making, processes, especially as it relates to peace and security are most visible during this period. Most peace building initiatives in this region and in particular peace negotiations are male dominated.

Chapter One
Historical Background and Women's Involvement in Peace Building

Mano River States

The Mano River region refers to the three countries which cover the river basin: Guinea, Liberia and Sierra Leone. The Mano River Union is an economic and trade union established in 1973 between Liberia and Sierra Leone, which Guinea joined in 1980. The Mano River Agreement of 1973 gives evidence that the three States can co-operate to revitalise and consolidate this common market and take measures to prevent conflict in the region. However, these efforts have been frustrated by the political instability and violent armed conflicts that have beset the region in the past decade, firstly in Liberia, followed by Sierra Leone.

The three countries are presently facing a tough challenge in resolving persisting political and security tensions within the sub-region and developing stable democracies. The violence is interwoven," an analyst for an international humanitarian organization explained. "War in Liberia begat war in Sierra Leone, which in turn begat attacks in Guinea and prolonged the civil war in Cote d'Ivoire. The recognized borders don't mean anything to many of the hardcore combatants. When a country finally achieves a peace treaty, the guys who make a living through the barrel of their guns seep across the border to the next country." (Jeff Drumtra, 2003) The root causes of the prolonged conflicts in the Mano River are attributed to interrelated internal and external factors such as bad governance, under development, gender inequalities, widespread poverty, and exploitation of natural resources or colonial legacy. The conflicts have directly impacted the lives and livelihoods of hundreds of thousands of the civilian populations, particularly women and children. The deliberate targeting of civilians has generated unprecedented levels of population displacement, with Guinea serving as a haven for refugees fleeing the conflicts in Liberia and Sierra Leone. For several consequent years, Guinea has been the host of the highest number of refugees in Africa.

Though internal in nature, the conflicts have taken a regional dimension as a result of ineffective disarmament of ex-combatants coupled with limited opportunities to transform them into productive citizens. The infiltration of rebels inside refugee camps is a threat to the security in the cross border areas. The increasing trade in small arms and ammunitions and the re-emerging conflicts in Liberia and Cote d'Ivoire exacerbate this situation. The socioeconomic situation of all three countries has deteriorated drastically and extreme poverty is widespread

Sierra Leone

Historical context

Sierra Leone is a West African country named by Portuguese explorers because of its peninsula mountains resembled a crouching lion. The country later became a British colony and gained independence during the period of pan African revolution in 1961. Post independence Sierra Leone was very unstable and showed signs of a future that occurred later. Coup attempt early in 1971 led to then Prime Minister Siaka Stevens calling in troops from neighbouring Guinea's army, which remained for two years. Stevens turned the government into a one-party state under the aegis of the All People's Congress Party in April 1978. In 1992 rebel soldiers overthrew Stevens's successor, Joseph Momoh, calling for a return to a multiparty system. In 1996, another military coup ousted the country's military leader and president.

Nevertheless, a multiparty presidential election proceeded in 1996, and People's Party candidate Ahmad Tejan Kabbah won with 59.4% of the vote, becoming Sierra Leone's first democratically elected president but a violent military coup ousted President Kabbah's civilian government in 1997. The leader of the coup, Lieut. Col. Johnny Paul Koroma, assumed the title Head of the Armed Forces Revolutionary Council (AFRC). Koroma began a reign of terror, destroying the economy and murdering enemies. The Commonwealth of Nations demanded the reinstatement of Kabbah, and ECOMOG, the Nigerian-led peacekeeping force, intervened. In 1998, after ten months in exile, Kabbah resumed his rule over Sierra Leone. The ousted junta and other rebel forces continued to wage attacks, many of which included the torture, rape, and brutal maimings of thousands of civilians, including countless children; amputation by machete was the horrific signature of the rebels. In addition to political power, the rebels, who were supported by Liberia's president Charles Taylor, sought control of Sierra Leone's rich diamond fields. In Jan. 1999, rebels and Liberian mercenaries stormed the capital, demanding the release of the imprisoned Revolutionary United Front (RUF) leader, Foday Sankoh. ECOMOG regained control of Freetown, but President Kabbah later released Sankoh so he could participate in peace negotiations. Pressured by Nigeria agreement in July 1999, this made Sankoh vice president of the country and in charge of the diamond mines. The accord dissolved in May 2000 after the RUF abducted about 500 UN peacekeepers and attacked Freetown, Sankoh was captured and died in government custody in 2003, while awaiting trial for war crimes.

Liberia

Historical context

Liberia is situated on the West Coast of Africa .Liberia is bounded on the north by the Republic of Guinea, on the west by the Republic of Sierra Leone, on the east by the Republic of Ivory Coast and on the south by the Atlantic Ocean. Much of West Africa's violence reaches back to the eruption of civil war in Liberia in late 1989. The region had no major refugee problems until that time. Liberians believed that their country partially founded by freed American slaves enjoyed a "special relationship" with the United States that would protect Liberia from the bloodshed prevalent elsewhere on the continent.

As the Liberian war quickly spiraled out of control in the early 1990s with ethnic massacres perpetrated by as many as 11 armed groups formed largely along ethnic lines, more than half of the country's three million people fled their homes. The main rebel force, led by Charles Taylor, controlled much of the countryside but failed to seize the capital, Monrovia.

West African peacekeeping troops—primarily from Nigeria—protected the capital and became active belligerents in the war.

As the military situation reached a stalemate in the mid-1990s, all sides grudgingly agreed to a cease-fire and national elections. Voters elected Taylor as president in 1997 after he threatened to resume the war if defeated at the polling booth. By 1999, nearly 90 percent of all Liberian refugees and displaced persons had returned home despite growing dismay at government corruption and human rights abuses. The international community condemned Taylor's government for its continued participation in Sierra Leone's civil war and its smuggling of Sierra Leonean diamonds.

A new rebel group known as Liberians United for Reconstruction and Development (LURD), dominated by ethnic Mandingos and using Guinea as a base, launched attacks in remote northern Liberia in 2000, provoking brutal countermeasures by Liberian government troops. A new wave of population displacement ensued as the LURD insurgency gained strength and reached the edge of Monrovia in mid-2003.

The Liberian Civil War, which was one of Africa's bloodiest, claimed the lives of more than 200,000 Liberians and further displaced a million others into refugee camps in neighbouring countries. An estimated 50,000 children were killed; many more were injured, orphaned, or abandoned.

On 11 August 2003 Liberian President Charles Taylor arrived in Nigeria, where he was granted asylum after he relinquished the Liberian presidency. Charles Taylor handed over power to his Vice-President Moses Blah in a historic ceremony, attended by the presidents.

Guinea

Historical context

Guinea was once a part of the great Mali Empire. Guinea became a French colony in 1890. After World War II, several labour parties were established, including the Parti Democratique de Guinee led by Ahmed Sekou Toure. Sekou Toure governed a one-party state and progressively developed strong dictatorial tendencies. He survived several attempted coups and continued to rule in Guinea until his death in 1984. Two weeks later, the military took control of the government and established the Second Guinean Republic under Lansana Conte. Presidential and parliamentary elections took place in late 1993 and Lansana Conte was declared president. He again won the presidential elections in 1998. The conflict in Guinea was a product of the volatile situation in the Mano River Union (MRU) region of West Africa. Guinea was in constant threat of being engulfed in the wars in Sierra Leone and Liberia (Human Rights Watch, 2001). Charles Taylor launched his rebellion in1989 very close to the Guinean border, in the mineral-rich area where Liberia, Guinea, Sierra Leone and the Ivory Coast meet. The threat to the stability of Guinea and the fighting along its borders led to a mass migration of people from the border communities.

Guinea in an attempt to restore stability led an intervention in Liberia to oust Charles Taylor. It became host to Liberian refugees to organize and recruit, and became the rear base for one of the armed movements known as Ulimo-K. The support to the refugees created a tension between President Taylor and the Guinean President Lansana Conte. Violence began to spread further into Guinea in 2000. At first there were hit-and-run raids, with the attackers coming across, killing civilians and burning villages, and then retreating back across the border, taking with them whatever they could loot. These attacks had one major effect, they turned the local Guinean population against the refugees living among them. Thus, the relationship between Liberia and Sierra Leonean refugees and their hosts in Guinea has been fraught with problems, which often led to violence.

Chapter Two

Role of women prior to the war

Women were disadvantaged and vulnerable prior to the outbreak of fighting in the Mano River States. Men were the sole breadwinners, whereas the women were caretakers of the home. They took care of needs like food, clothes, school fees and medicine. The average woman was financially handicapped and tried to make ends meet by engaging in petty trading, market gardening, food processing and other income-generating activities. About 15% of women in the urban area were engaged in professional careers in secretarial work, teaching, nursing, NGO activities, banking and civil service (clerical jobs). Thus while some were able to live comfortably, and provide for their families, others struggled to get even one meal a day. By and large, although women worked long hours in diverse activities, they were undervalued.

In the rural areas, women did the bulk of the heavy work, in such pursuits as farming, market gardening or agriculture. Women sowed swamp rice, groundnuts, cassava, potatoes and vegetables. Women were rarely involved in decision-making, they were subject to hostile laws, and many of them, particularly the illiterate ones, were victims of domestic and sexual violence. Women were also discriminated against with regard to enrolment in educational institutions, property ownership, and social status. They lacked access to information, health and other social facilities. They were merely seen as child bearers and property to be inherited by their husbands' family at his death. They were completely unaware of their strategic needs and roles in society. Consequently, they had little say in social, economic and political development. Men held positions of power at all levels of society. They held the key positions as politicians, government ministers, heads of departments, parastatals and they were generally more educated than women.

Effects of the conflict on Women

The war drastically changed women's traditional roles. The women in the displaced camps became the breadwinners of their family. This diversity of women's experiences in conflict and post-conflict situations challenges the conventional image of women as passive and helpless victims of war. In addition to becoming combatants, women challenge traditional gender stereotypes by taking over traditional male occupations and responsibilities (Afshar, H., and Eade, D, 2004). Most of the men were killed or became displaced; as a result 60% of the homes are female-headed households.

Some women were more desperate to survive during the war. One woman described to me how women became prostitutes, Commanding Officer's (CO) wives (rebels commanders wives), soldiers/fighters, slaves (those that were taken forcibly from their villages were used for any purpose), agents for fighters (went on reconnaissance missions for warring factions), coal miners (burn charcoal for sale), Civilian CO (spokes persons for civilians during the war. Whenever there was a problem between fighters and civilians, CO served as mediator, mostly females occupied this position.

Women's experiences during the war reveal the true horror that last a decade. The worst of these experiences are recorded in rural communities where women came in direct contact with rebel, government and peacekeeping forces (ECOMOG). The Mano River women who were already a disadvantaged class prior to the war, lost the protection of the male family members during the violence, many of them became widowed or separated.

Women were raped continually during the violence by all sides and the results are "ECOMOG babies", rebel babies etc. Forced impregnation and forced pregnancy can be used to deepen the humiliation and to produce babies of the ethnicity of the rapists. (Human Right Watch, 1999). Many women live in fear that though the war is over the fathers of these babies might return. Reintegration of ex-combatants, saw many of the combatants who had raped, assaulted and victimized these women moving back to the communities they terrorized. Many have retained an aura of intimidation and who have been traumatized have to face some of their attackers on a daily basis.

Many young girls, who spent the war serving as wives and girlfriends to combatants, later became prostitutes and lobbied for clientele among the peacekeepers. There is always the threat that Sexually Transmitted infections (STIs), and HIV/AIDS, are on the rise. Women in both rural and urban communities display signs of Post Traumatic Stress Disorder, women suffer from insomnia, paranoia, anxiety, and hyper vigilance. Many victims of rape, particularly those who were young girls of 11 – 13 years old, suffer from lasting effects of the experiences.

There is also disagreement as to why women become combatants, some state for material gain, to protect their children/ family, some see it as a profession, some were forced (during forceful recruitment the soldiers often used terms like "you good to go" "you have good body for holding gun"), saw it as a way of gaining recognition, for fear of being raped. Others joined to embarrass other girls by giving them load to carry and giving them to men for sex. After the war, a stigma remained with women who were combatants, they were tagged: killers, man-woman, militia, lovers of material things, men lappers, "join soldiers".

Majority of the female combatants still have a war mentality. They continue to have intimidating attitudes, many are still addicted to drugs and worst of all, now that the war is over their parents, and other immediate family members are their victims.

Another effect is the increase in the number of refugees in Neighbouring countries. During the conflict, many women in the urban areas were able to leave and seek refuge in neighbouring countries in West Africa, or in the Western world.

Religion also plays a key role in the lives of most of the women from both communities. Those who were Christians said they prayed fervently that God would divinely intervene and save them. There were ironic experiences of women who were atheists prior to the war but were during mass killings in their communities, they were somehow spared or managed to escape and this caused them to believe in the existence in a supernatural being that had spared them. There were also examples of women who stopped trusting their faith, as they believed that "a good God, would not have allowed the war to happen" A young lady said to me during my meeting with the Community Empowerment Organisation of Liberia "every time I hear the name of God I get very angry, I don't have any faith in him any more".

The war had an ironic positive effect on the Mano River women; many women became more vocal, large numbers of women joined groups, associations and NGOs aimed at building peace. Given women's traditional responsibility in most societies as day-today caregivers for their families and communities, the impact of conflict has distinct consequences based on gender (Cockburn 2001b).

Chapter Three
Women's Role in Peace building

Women contributes to the peace process by promoting education about basic civil rights and responsibilities, encouraging those who would listen not to join in but to pray and work hard, providing education and disciplining children in the extended family so they would not get involved in the conflict. Mobilizing and sensitizing women and communities about the dangers of violence and the need for self-reliance through training, prayer and talking about it. Advocating for basic rights, especially for women and children, involving in peace education and conflict resolution activities. Preaching forgiveness to victims to encourage them not to seek revenge, preaching love and talked about Jesus. Organising sensitization workshops on peace building, and working with community groups to disseminate message of peace. Networking with other agencies and partners on the campaign against violence. When the war intensified there was awareness-raising, advocacy, lobbying, peace education and mass education which led to the formation of the Mano River Women's Peace Network (MARWOPNET). An organisation set up by Mano River Women to address the devastating condition of their countries.

The MARWOPNET promoted affirmative action as an important strategy in bringing about transformation using the help line and monitoring reports from human rights groups. They were involved in peace negotiations. Coping skill centers were established. As a result of their growing confidence they were able to actually confront the rebels and stand firm against the ruling military junta in 1996, forcing them to call elections for a democratically elected government and sent out petitions. MARWOPNET women also continue to research conditions in sprawling refugee camps and conduct leadership training for women working in local peace groups and at the community level. As important as their high-level approaches to political leaders, the MARWOPNET women travel the country, going into villages and huts and speaking directly to women about what they need to rebuild their lives, whether more rice or more counselling (Eliza Griswold, 2002).

In 2003, the Mano River Women's Peace Network (MARWOPNET) was awarded the United Nations Prize for Human Rights by the United Nations General Assembly in recognition of its outstanding achievement in the promotion of human rights, including women's rights. (UN Prize for Human Rights, 2003). Today, as a post-war strategy, MARWOPNET and many local NGOs are embarking on training programs in conflict prevention, conflict management, conflict resolution and peace building, countrywide. In the rural areas, more grassroots women became aware of the need to protect their children from sexual and domestic violence and have become activists for this cause.

Chapter Four
The Importance of Women's Involvement in Peace Building

"Women have sacrificed their lives for peace. They have challenged militarism and urged reconciliation over retribution. They have contributed to peace building as activists, as community leaders, as survivors of the most cataclysmic horrors of war. They have transformed peace processes on every continent by organizing across political, religious and ethnic affiliations. But their efforts are rarely supported or rewarded". (Sir Leaf, E.J. 2002). The 1995 Beijing Platform for Action (Par.142a) emphasizes the need to 'promote equal opportunities for women to participate in all forums and peace activities at all levels, particularly at the decision-making levels' and the need to 'strengthen the role of women and to ensure representation of women at all decision-making levels in national and international institutions which may make or influence policy with regard to matters related to peace-keeping, preventative diplomacy, and related activities in all stages of peace mediation and negotiation'. Earlier in October 2000, the UN Security Council adopted the groundbreaking Resolution 1325 on women, peace and security that calls on all actors to take "measures that support local women's peace initiatives and indigenous processes for conflict resolution, and that involve women in all implementation mechanisms of the peace agreements" (UN Resolution 1325, 2000). For the first time in the UN history, Resolution 1325 acknowledges the contribution of women as peace makers and agents of change for peace beyond their status of victims of armed conflicts and enables women's organizations to gain leverage on getting access to official peace negotiations. However, in spite of all these progresses, we are forced to recognize that women are not systematically involved in peace processes and that obstacles to their participation are numerous. Official peace processes in the Mano River States remain an almost exclusively male domain, and little has been done to encourage women's equal participation. This glaring lack of Mano River women in main stream peace building must be urgently addressed based not only on the fundamental principle of the equality between men and women, but also on the dire need for the new perspectives and unique experiences that women can bring.

Despite the notable absence of women in formal peace processes and mechanisms, Mano River women have been actively involved in informal peace building initiatives and have used methods that have created an enabling environment for some level of sustainable peace at the grassroots and national levels. "Women, who know the price of conflict so well, are also better equipped than men to prevent or resolve it. For generations, women have served as peace educators, both in their families and in their societies. They have proved instrumental in building bridges rather than walls." (UN Secretary-General Kofi Annan, October 2000). Women have been active in mobilizing communities, creating opportunities for dialogue and non-violent means of conflict resolution, as well as mending the ripped fabric of society. While women's reliance on their gender based roles offers them an opportunity to participate in peace processes, it considerably limits their potential as peacemakers beyond their communities. To be truly effective, women need to participate in all aspects and all levels planning, implementation, maintenance, monitoring, and evaluation of conflict resolution and peace building processes. (Ernest A, 1998)

Women in conflict zones in the Mano River States have thus been mobilizing and asserting their right to fully participate in a process that has important consequences on all aspects of their lives. In contrast, women look at it not as an opportunity for personal political advancement, but as a chance to heal the wounds of the affected society for the betterment of all. Women focus on issues that make a difference to human lives and realities, not to their own careers. Women bring very different perspectives to peace negotiations because they tend to articulate peace in terms of meeting human safety needs and other aspects of well-being. Their vision of peace entails not only the absence of war, but also the absence of explicit and implicit violence and oppressive structures at a personal, structural, and cultural level, as well as a just social system and economic, social, cultural, spiritual, and emotional well-being for all(UNICEF, 1999).

MARWOPNET understanding of peace as a human well being lead them to viable solutions to peace building. While the Peace processes tend concentrate on issues of power and historical grievances, even though these women acknowledged the importance of these processes, feel that the quality of life is a more crucial matter. "We explicitly recognise the particular and distinctive peacemaking roles played by women in conflict afflicted communities. Women and women's organisations are often reservoirs of important local capacities which can be used in peace-building activities" (International Alert, 1998). Women highlight the human consequences of violence and armed conflict. They emphasize the importance of understanding and addressing the root causes of conflict as a way of promoting sustainable Peace.

They add value to peace negotiations by bringing in practical understanding of the problems faced by civilian populations as well as tangible and effective solutions and approaches for addressing them. Therefore, by ensuring that peace accords signed during negotiations correspond to the daily realities and needs on the ground, women advance prospects for sustainable peace.

Chapter Five
Conclusion

The inclusion of women is particularly important in peace promotion because sustainable peace, justice, and freedom from violence cannot be achieved as long as individual persons or groups, in particular women, are excluded or marginalized. Thus, all governmental and nongovernmental actors and society at large have a responsibility to make concrete steps towards gender equality and translate the constitutional gender equality into reality by implementing measures that promote the advancement of women and their rights.

Overall, a culture of sustainable peace requires that fundamental human rights as well as women's rights at legal, political, social, and economic levels are recognized and upheld. This includes honoring and implementing of all Conventions against gender based violence and other international human rights instruments. The Mano River States government and society must therefore recognize that violations of women's rights in times of war are an extension of the gender based abuses they encounter in peace time. This cycle of violence cannot be eliminated until peacetime violence, especially the abuses is addressed.

Another prerequisite for sustainable peace is fundamental social transformation, which reforms the socialization processes and changes the societal structures that uphold and reinforce patriarchal ideology and gender inequality.

Therefore, it is important to use a gender sensitive lens to thoroughly examine and redefine existing social institutions, from the family to the state apparatus, because they all perpetuate gender discrimination. This, in addition to being a violation of women's human rights, is the most formidable barrier to women's effective participation in the peace processes. Ultimately, women's equal participation, their perspectives, knowledge, and experiences are all crucial to the creation of a more just, prosperous, and peaceful Mano River States.

Chapter Six
References

Anderlini, S. N., 2000, Women at the Peace Table: Making a Difference, New York, United Nations Development Fund for Women (UNIFEM).

Arimiebi Ekiyor Thelma., 2002, Women's Empowerment in Peace building: A Platform for Involvement in Decision-making, The WIPNET Experience.

Afshar, H., & Eade, D. (Eds.). (2004). Development, women, and war. Oxford: Oxfam GB. Turshen, M., & Twagiramariya, C. (Eds.). (1998). What women do in wartime. London and New York: Zed Books Ltd.

Best practices in peace-building and non-violent conflict resolution: some documented African women's peace initiatives. (1998). Inter-agency document prepared and edited by Ernest, A. for UNHCR, UNESCO, UNDP, UNFPA, & UNIFEM. http://www.peacewomen.org/resources/Organizing/BestPractices1998.pdf

Caroline O N Moser and Fiona C Clark 2001, Victims, Perpetrators or Actors? Zed Books

Cockburn, Cynthia, 2001b, "The Gendered Dynamics of Armed Conflict and Political Violence." In Caroline Moser and Fiona C. Clark, eds. Victims, Perpetrators or Actors? Gender, Armed Conflict and Political Violence. London: Zed Books.

Coker Patrick, March 2003, Sierra Leone – Building the Road to Recovery, Institute for Security Studies, Monograph no 80.

Coomaraswamy, Radhika, 2001, Report of the Special Rapporteur on violence against women, its causes and consequences, submitted in accordance with Commission on Human Rights resolution, Ref E/CN.4/2002/83/Add.2.

El-Bushra, J. and Piza Lopez, E., 1993,'Development in conflict; the gender dimension', Report of an Oxfam AGRA fast Workshop held in Pattaga Thailand, 1-4th February 1993, Oxfam Uk/1-ACORD

Eliza Griswold, 2002, From village street to presidential palace, the Mano River network helps heal the wounds of a brutal war., Ford Foundation Report http://www.fordfound.org/publications/ff_report/view_ff_report_detail.cfm?report_index=364.

Empowerment, gender and peace promotion, 2004, Focus on Gender and Peace building Newsletter, 3/04. http://www.cfd-ch.org/pdfs/newsletter3_04_egl.pdf

Femmes Africa Solidarité, 1997, Women's Participation in the Peace Process in Sierra Leone, Femmes Africa Solidarité.

Human Rights Watch, July 1999, Getting Away with Murder, Mutilation, Rape, New Testimony from Sierra Leone, , Vol.11 No 3(A) http://www.hrw.org/reports/1999/sierra/.

International Alert, July 1998, Code of Conduct

Jalloh, Alpha, 2002, Bring Media to the People, World Press Review (VOL. 49, No. 6); Free Town, Sierra Leone June.

Jeff Drumtra, 2003, West Africa's Refugee Crisis Spills Across Many, http://www.migrationinformation.org/feature/print.cfm?ID=148

Lata Narayanaswamy and Charlie Sever, November 2004, Gender-Based Violence – What is the significance for development interventions? BRIDGE, Development-Gender

Mano River Women's Peace Network (MARWOPNET), Voices of Peace, online Journal.

Mazurana Dyan and Carlson Kristopher, 2004, From Combat to Community; Women and Girls of Sierra Leone, Women waging peace.

Nadine Puechguirbal, 2004, "Involving women in peace processes: lessons learnt from four African countries (Burundi, DRC, Liberia and Sierra Leone), in Gender and Peace-Building in Africa, Training for Peace, Norwegian Institute of International Affairs, Oslo, pp. 47-66.

Pankhurst, D, August 2000, Women, Gender and Peace Building, Centre for Conflict Resolution Working Paper, Department of Peace Studies, University of Bradford.

Rehn, E., & Sirleaf, E.J. 2002, Women, war and peace: the independent experts' assessment on the impact of armed conflict on women and women's role in peace-building. http://www.unifem.org/index.php?f_page_pid=149

Sierra Leone, Info please" http://www.infoplease.com/ipa/A0107959.html

Swanee Hunt and Cristina Posa May-June 2001, Women Waging Peace, Foreign Policy, No. 124, pp. 38-47.

The African Women's Development Fund (AWDF), 2003, Report from Community Empowerment Program, Paynesville, Liberia.

The African Women's Development Fund (AWDF), 2005, Report from Kailahun District Women in Development, Kailahun District, Sierra Leone.

The African Women Development Fund (AWDF), 2004, Report from Liberian Refugee Women Organisation (LIREWO), Accra, Ghana.

The African Women Development Fund (AWDF), 2004, Report from Liberia Women Initiative, Monrovia, Liberia.

The African Women Development Fund (AWDF), 2004, Report from Sierra Leone Women Forum, Freetown, Sierra Leone.

The African Women Development Fund, 2003, 2004 and 2005, Site Visit Report Liberia, Sierra Leone and Guinea Conakry, conducted by Ndey Jobarteh, Senior Programs Manager.

United Nations Declaration on the Elimination of Violence against Women, 1994, A/C.3/48/1.5,23, art. 1.

United Nations Educational, Scientific, and Cultural Organization. (1999). The women's agenda for a culture of peace in Africa. Women Organize for Peace and Non-Violence in Africa: Pan-African Women's Conference on a Culture of Peace. Zanzibar, United Republic of Tanzania, May 17-20, 1999.

United Nations, Women, Peace and Security, Study submitted by the Secretary-General pursuant to Security Council resolution 1325 (2000).

UNAIDS Report 1998

UNIFEM, 2001, "Engendering Peace, Reflections on the Burundi Peace Process", African Women for Peace Series.

USAID, 2007, Women and Conflict.